Boys and Girls Come Out to Play

Not better or worse, just different

by

Ros Bayley and Sally Featherstone

"Boys and girls seem to determine and arrive at a common goal in different ways."
Making Learning Visible; children as individual and group learners Project Zero, Reggio Children

Reprinted 2010
Published 2009 by A&C Black Publishers Limited
36 Soho Square, London W1D 3QY
www.acblack.com

First published in the UK by Featherstone Education Limited 2005

ISBN 978-1-9050-1917-5

Text © Sally Featherstone and Ros Bayley 2005
Series Editor Sally Featherstone
Cover photograph © Shutterstock

Printed in Great Britain by Latimer Trend & Company Limited

This book is produced using paper that is made from wood grown in
managed, sustainable forests. It is natural, renewable and recyclable.
The logging and manufacturing processes conform to the environmental
regulations of the country of origin.

To see our full range of titles
visit www.acblack.com

Introduction

"Our approach to gender relationships in early years settings sometimes hardens rather than challenge stereotypical behaviour. This approach is characterised by the corrective and sometimes punitive form of response offered to active young boys in counterpoint to the celebratory response given to compliant and passive young girls playing in the home corner or at the writing table. Both these responses should give us cause for concern." Penny Holland

A young boy on holiday crouches beside a table in a beach-side cafe. In his hands are two realistic looking toy dinosaurs, a Tyrannosaurus Rex and a smaller plant eater. The boy carefully scoops sand and forms it into a landscape, rushing off regularly to fetch driftwood and pebbles to make the scene more lifelike. When satisfied with the scene, he begins to play. The tyrannosaurus rears on its hind legs and stalks its prey, eventually crashing on the other dinosaur's back and rolling over as it devours its meal. This is accompanied by an appropriate sound track! The boy's mother frequently leans over to tell her son to keep the noise down, stop getting in the way of the waiters, stop rushing around. His father glances frequently at his son, but says nothing. The boy is so involved in his game that he hears nothing, and has to be physically removed to his chair when his meal arrives. During the meal he looks frequently at his scene and at one point leaves his chair to rearrange the dinosaurs so they appear to be sleeping. As soon as he has finished eating he returns to the game, the soundtrack starts again and he is completely involved.

Two days later, the same beach cafe. A young girl is sitting at the table with her family. She has a tyrannnosaurus too! However, it is different and so is her game. The toy is a soft stuffed creature, realistic in colour and features, and obviously newly acquired. The girl always puts the dinosaur on all four feet, never in the aggressive position of back feet only. When another family member raises the dinosaur on its back feet she simply returns it to all fours. This is how she plays. The dinosaur is first given the shiny metal table number to look in as a mirror; then the girl takes a hair decoration from her own hair and puts it round the dinosaur's neck. The dinosaur remains on the table throughout the meal. It walks (on all fours) to see other members of the family. It is fed (spaghetti and ice cream). It is wrapped in a table napkin and rocked to sleep. It is frequently hugged and kissed. The girl never leaves her chair, and her behaviour is greeted with warmth and approval by everyone.

The story is true, the two children were Spanish. The language is immaterial - the gender issues are universal and are the subject of this book.

So what is happening?

'From infancy boys prefer mechanical or structural toys, girls prefer soft, cuddly toys. Boys' stories are filled with excitement and action, girls' stories pay attention to human dynamics. Boys are primarily interested in objects and things, girls in people and relationships. Boys use dolls for attack weapons and warfare, girls use dolls for playing out domestic scenes."

condensed from *Boys and Girls Learn Differently* Michael Gurian

So what was happening on those days in Spain? Do boys always use toys in active, aggressive, realistic ways? Do girls always use toys in domestic and sedentary ways? And if so, what makes them behave in the ways they do?

'Boys and Girls Come Out to Play' explores some of the issues we are now facing in supporting both boys and girls in their earliest years and ensuring that we and they know that 'boys and girls are not better or worse than each other, they are just different'.

In writing this book we have focused on a range of aspects of children's lives and learning.

- What happens before birth to affect the development of boys and girls?
- What do we now know about the growth and development of the brain in young children?
- What are our existing assumptions about gender and behaviour?
- What do we know about the differences between boys and girls in:

    physical growth

    cognitive development

    concentration, motivation and interest

    language development

    social development and relationships

    the expectations of society and the education system

    the affect of role models

    the influence of the media

and how does this knowledge inform us in early years settings? What should we be doing? How should we be working? What are the essentials of a setting that encourages both boys and girls to be the best they can be?

The race to make a brain

100,000,000,000 BRAIN CELLS -
GIRL BABY HAS EARLY ADVANTAGE IN BRAIN RACE

A girl embryo gestated and lodged in her mother's womb begins her epic journey genetically programmed to become a female. In the first three months her genetic makeup ignores the effects of **hormones, including testosterone** flooding through the womb at this time, and her body continues to develop female characteristics (this is why some scientists claim that all foetuses are female!).

The two sides of the baby's cortex (the part of her brain that makes her human) develop at different rates. The right develops more quickly than the left. This right half handles movement, emotion and a sense of space - sometimes called 'the big picture' hemisphere. As the later blooming left side of the brain begins to develop, (this is the side that deals with language and detail - 'the parts of the whole') the growing baby begins to make links between the left and right sides of her brain.

The neutral response to early testosterone may be giving girls an advantage here. While boy babies are concentrating their energy on growing more muscles, extra bone and a bigger body, girls are busy growing their brains!

Individual brain cells (**neurons**) reach out to link with others as the baby grows, giving instructions, collecting information and responding to experiences, to movement and to stress (be that excessive noise, violent motion or the stress of her mother).

Some brain cells make connections with the other side of the brain, using the fibrous link between the two halves of the brain, called the **corpus callosum**. This enables the baby girl to begin using both sides of her brain together, and may make her **better at language and reading expressions, more interested in people and relationships**.

100,000,000,000 BRAIN CELLS -
BOY BABY DISADVANTAGED BY TESTOSTERONE

A boy embryo gestated and lodged in his mother's womb begins his epic journey genetically programmed to become a male. During the first three months his genetic makeup reacts to the frequent floods of **testosterone** in the womb. Chemical effects trigger changes in his physical growth - making heavier bones, bigger muscles, more red blood cells and male genitalia and suppressing female characteristics. The chemical effects also triggered changes in the structure of his brain (changes now known to be visible even to the naked eye) making his thinking and brain development different from females.

The right side of this baby's cortex (the part of his brain that makes him human) also develops more quickly than the left, But that important late blooming left side (the language and reasoning half) **develops even more slowly than in girls**.

As individual brain cells in his right hemisphere begin to reach out for other cells, his left hemisphere is less ready to receive them than in a girl. The corpus callosum is thinner and smaller, and although at birth this boy will probably have as many links between cells as a girl has, the links will be in the separate halves of the brain, and most will be in the right side,

This pattern will have an effect on his behaviour and thinking for the rest of his life. It will potentially make him **better at maths and spatial problem solving, more interested in machines and technology** than most girls.

Boys are also much **more likely to suffer brain damage** at birth, more likely to have **delayed speech or dyslexia**, more likely to be **restless and slower to gain fine motor control** than <u>most</u> girls.

However, we must realise that: 'There are many more differences between children of the same sex than between the sexes. If we lined up all the boys and all girls on the basis of almost any characteristic, there would be lots more overlap than difference attributable to only one gender.'

Your Child's Growing Mind Jane Healey

Before birth

"Sex hormones are especially potent because they can physically shape a male or female brain and influence its skills, favouring such things as language in females and spatial abilities - mathematical concepts, for example - in males."

Inside the Brain Ronald Kotulak

It has been said that all embryos are female, but this is not strictly true. All embryos have the genetic makeup to be either male or female; their genes will decide which. The first three months of pregnancy are hugely influential in determining both the sex and the gender of each embryo. We go on later to explain the differences between sex and gender.

The latest documentation on the 'before birth' stage indicates that in the womb, potentially female embryos have an advantage, and the description opposite is an attempt to give a simple explanation of how. During the first crucial months of pregnancy, surges of testosterone flood the womb. The testosterone has a markedly more dramatic effect on embryos destined to be boys. Boy embryos are triggered into developing the physical attributes of males - their sexual organs, more blood cells, about one third more muscle bulk, heavier bones and other physical features. They also develop the unique features of a male brain.

> "So you make a boy brain out of a girl brain at about the same time in pre-natal development when the two hemispheres have their greatest difference in growth."
>
> Judy Lauter, University of Oklahoma Health Science Centre

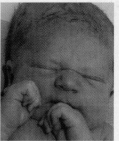

It seems that this diversion of the male embryo's energy to physical development may have an effect on the growth of other organs, particularly the brain. The chemical surge and the subsequent concentration on physical development comes at the time when there is the most difference in the development of the two hemispheres of the brain. The right hemisphere develops first, the left hemisphere (the one that deals with language and detail) develops later, and is at a crucial stage when energy is diverted to physical changes. Judy Lauter also says there is a possibility that during this period things can go wrong with the left hemisphere, including an increased rate of language problems in boys - stuttering, dyslexia and language delay.

We must remember that the hormone flood in the uterus affects each child differently. It is possible for some female embryos to be slightly affected by the testosterone surges, and they may develop some masculine characteristics, just as it is possible for some boy embryos to be less affected than the average males and develop some feminine characteristics.

Male/female; Feminine/masculine

Sexual identity is in the perineum, gender identity is in the brain.

The behaviour of these boys is on the extreme of boy behaviour - active, noisy, rushing round in groups.
They are:
male sex
masculine gender

and this child?
What is his/her sex?
What is her/his gender?
Many children (and adults) have clearly defined sex, but a much greater mixture of gender characteristics.

The behaviour of these girls is on the extreme of girl behaviour - sociable, quiet, full of detail and language.
They are:
female sex
feminine gender

Think of your own identity. Where would you be on this spectrum? What is the balance between masculine and feminine in your personal makeup? What about your partner, your mother or father, your manager?

The balance between sex and gender

"The historical causation of gender differences in the brain probably goes back to hunter/gatherer society and continues in our high population culture, but the logistical causation of brain differences lies in how male and female hormones influence development."
Boys and Girls Learn Differently Michael Gurian

The descriptions and views on previous pages may have puzzled you. You may know children and adults who are nothing like the extremes described - these may be boys who enjoy home play, stories and playing in groups with girls; and girls who are the first out of the door into the garden, noisy, boisterous and sometimes a bit clumsy, Of course this is true - as Jane Healey says:

'There are many more differences between children of the same sex than between the sexes.'

The difference between sex and gender has been defined thus:

> **Sex** is the biological/functional difference between male and female. It is defined by the genes in our chromosomes, fixed at conception and determining our sexuality (male or female).

> **Gender** is more complex. It is a psychological term describing our awareness and reaction to our biological sex, and is affected by biological, psychological and social factors resulting in characteristics that are either masculine or feminine.

Of course, some of our gender related reactions are unconscious, some are learned, some result from the expectations of our families or the society in which we live. Some are consciously 'learned' because we wish to impress our friends, keep our partners happy, give us a quiet life, or because we wish to change our behaviour as a reaction to thought, philosophy, professional practice or changing times. And at times we all feel a real tension between our natural response to events or people and 'political correctness' or socially acceptable norms. A real tension for adolescents has always been between the behaviour adopted by their contemporaries and the behaviour expected by adults!

The young children we work with have tensions too. On one hand our society expects 'boys to be boys' and 'girls to sit nicely' (Penny Holland); on the other hand we want girls to grow up strong and boys to grow up sensitive to the needs of others. This must be very confusing for young children, who may be getting different messages about their behaviour from parents, peers, practitioners and the media.

Existing attitudes and assumptions

What do we expect of boys and girls? Are our expectations the same for both, and do our expectations change with experience, age, culture or situation? In a recent article in The Times newspaper, reflecting on the arrival of a second son when she was hoping for a daughter, Alison Cameron said:

> 'This was no fleeting romantic pang of regret. It was a deep, dark sense of mourning for the parent I would never be, and specifically it was a longing for my blue eyed Charlotte Lillee. I would never be her role model, the one who helped her to find her place in the world, the voice in her ear telling her she could be anything she wanted to be.'

The majority of early years practitioners are women; most women (and many men) would empathise with Alison's feelings of loss. Women understand the needs of girls, they understand how girls react; their deep and instinctive interest in people and how they relate to each other; their natural disposition to quiet activities, domestic play and story making; their earlier development in the understanding and use of language; their generally compliant nature. These assumptions are not just present in early years settings, they are assumptions of our society.

On the other hand, for many women, boys are a mystery! A frequent response to boys' behaviour is 'If only they could be more like girls!' The girls who find it easier to sit still, who watch adults (and other girls) closely, learn quickly how to behave and respond, particularly in social or group situations. Learning 'girl like' behaviour would make life much less complex for adults, and as a result would be encouraged and rewarded.

But boys make life difficult and complicated. They are often lively and noisy, they are risk takers and experimenters, they are more interested in things than in people, and they resist our attempts to make them more like girls. Their additional muscle bulk and red blood cells make boys restless and fidgety, their slower development of writing and reading skills frustrate our 'catch up' schemes, their yearning to be outside, all combine to make boy behaviour a 'problem' not a blessing.

Existing attitudes and assumptions

"If we compel children throughout our culture to to sit down and shut up or speak only when spoken to, then we create a kind of child who does somewhat well without physical education or recess. But since our culture values freedom in a child's emotional expression, and given that we want the brain to actually be better at *varied* learning, academic and social skills, our classrooms must include an outdoor component where the body can breathe so the mind can grow."

Boys and Girls Learn Differently Michael Gurian

And of course, these assumptions influence our opinion of <u>all</u> boys, whatever their place on the gender continuum. We have such fixed assumptions about boys' behaviour that we sometimes forget their positive behaviours and qualities. Boys are honest, straightforward and frank. They love taking risks, pressing buttons, trying things out, testing everything they experience - even adults. Our assumption is that boys will be active and noisy, and when they are, we criticise them We don't expect boys to be generous, thoughtful or sensitive, and when they are, we cynically call them 'soft'. We secretly admire the man who disproves our assumptions by buying flowers or cleaning the bathroom, but we dismiss their behaviour as 'untypical'.

Our assumptions about girls are just as much part of our society. We expect girls to be submissive, well behaved and compliant, and these are qualities of many girls. But when our assumptions are challenged by girls who are strong, independent thinkers and leaders, we are surprised into thinking of them as unusual. We greet these behaviours with puzzlement and concern. We perhaps label such girls as 'rebellious' or 'difficult' instead of recognising that some girls are showing us that girls <u>can</u> be different, and some are learning to be more like boys.

Their behaviour may be a response to the feeling that boys get the most attention, appear to do the most interesting things, care less about what adults think of them, rush about with their friends, climb, run, jump and swing in risky ways. This must seem very attractive to some girls, and some will begin to model their behaviour on the boys they admire.

So within each group of children, there are boys and girls who match our assumptions and expectations, but there are others who should make us stop and think, reconsidering both our assumptions and the needs of both sexes and all genders. Each child has a unique mixture of characteristics, and all children observe others and copy their behaviours.

Existing attitudes and assumptions

Behaviour which makes us reflect on our assumptions and challenge stereotypical views should be welcomed. It is through reflection that assumptions change and the expectations of society are modified. Early Years practitioners have a powerful role to play in changing attitudes, behaviours and expectations in both children and adults. Despite current claims that we are eroding the differences in adult opportunities for men and women, you only need to watch children's TV on Saturday morning to see the difference between the programmes and particularly the adverts aimed at boys and those aimed at girls. Advert breaks include messages from fast food companies, where boys and girls play in different ways with different 'free gifts'. Boys run, fly, swoop with their toys, while girls sit quietly, carefully positioning dolls, playing with ponies, dressing up with beads and makeup. These adverts aimed at young children continue to emphasise the view of many adults that 'boys will be boys and girls will sit nicely.'

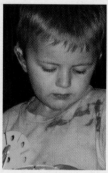

This is untrue and unfair to both sexes. The assumption that boys are unfeeling has now been disproved by research indicating that in fact many boys may feel more deeply than girls; they are just not expected to show it. The view that girls are quiet and submissive has been disproved by research which demonstrates that girls are becoming much more assertive, much more 'boy like'.

Despite years of guidance, practice and even legislation in equality of opportunity, the attitudes to boys and girls and the behaviours we expect have only resulted in an attempt to make boys and girls the same. Making sure children have a fair share of the wheels in the Lego, turns using the computer and opportunities to dress up or play with dolls, only ensures equality of <u>access</u>, not true equality of opportunity. We now need to refocus and ensure real equality by understanding the needs of boys <u>and</u> girls; their differences as well as their similarities; the different ways they learn; the different ways their brains develop. Only when we can honestly say that every girl and every boy has their individual needs catered for, will we be able to say we have achieved equality of <u>opportunity</u>.

Alison Cameron concludes her article (first quoted on page 8) with this thought:

> 'Boys have a serene beauty that I can't find in the faces of girls, who seem merely pretty to me. I now see life as an adventure of newness. This is not some repeat of my own childhood, but a strange and exciting land. I am the mother of boys and I am going to show them that they have the world at their feet.'

We should be just as prepared to challenge <u>our</u> assumptions.

Existing attitudes and assumptions

Our assumptions about the behaviour and development of boys and girls are so deep rooted in our society and behaviour that it is sometimes difficult to be objective about what we DO think. Our assumptions are influenced consciously and sub-consciously. They are shaped by our families and friends, by our upbringing, our culture, religion, social circle, by the people we admire, including role models from the media. We are also influenced subconsciously by advertisements, by images on posters and in magazines, overheard conversations, staffroom gossip, books we read, even by the soundtrack on TV programmes and the adverts that punctuate them.

Sometimes we consciously adapt our views, change our language, challenge our own or others' assumptions, sometimes our views are changed over time by what others say and do. Sometimes we change by reflecting on our own behaviour, by changing our policies or by following a directive from someone else. However it is evident that our assumptions are very difficult to change because we feel so emotionally close to them.

Our assumptions about boys and girls are deeply embedded in our lives and our behaviours. We assume that we know how boys and girls behave. We assume we know what is best for them and we construct a society and an education system which is built on a shared set of assumptions developed over time. Policies and procedures change very slowly, and the assumptions they are built on may need to be challenged in the light of new knowledge.

Of course we want the best for all children, regardless of their sex or gender characteristics. Girls need our support in becoming braver, stronger and more assertive. Boys need our support in acknowledging their feelings, understanding the needs of others and feeling OK about adopting and accepting 'softer' behaviour in others and in themselves. In doing this, we may need to courageously challenge some of the assumptions which have become embedded in our society and in the education and care systems.

Overleaf we explore some common assumptions about boys and girls, and feminine and masculine behaviours.

Some common assumptions

Assumption 1: We should try to make boys and girls equal by making them the same.
This intention was at the heart of the philosophy of 'give everyone the same opportunities and you will make them equal'. It confused equality of opportunity (equivalence for each) and equity of access (experiencing the curriculum). The more we learn about brain development in children, the more we realise that boys and girls learn in <u>different</u> ways, and need <u>different</u> sorts of support. True equality can only come through recognition and acceptance of the differences, and provision for different learning styles and needs.

Assumption 2: Boys and girls learn in the same way and in a predictable order.
This is clearly not true. Everything we now know about the development of both boys and girls tells us that there are distinct differences in the way the brain develops in each. The differences are genetic, and experiences and expectations before and after birth combine to accentuate them.

Assumption 3: If you want to achieve in life, learn to read and write as early as possible.
Children learn to read and write when their brains are mature enough to decode the print and their bodies are mature enough to manage writing tools. They also learn to read when reading is seen by them to be important and interesting. Maturity of these features of the brain and the body happen at different times in boys and girls. Many girls are ready to begin the complex task of reading and writing at about four and a half; many boys need much longer, and for some boys readiness does not really arrive until around eight.

Of course, good practitioners know it is possible to support earlier readiness by offering boys writing activities which extend their skills and capture their interests without risking failure. The best way to help all children to become readers and writers is to inspire and excite them with the possibilities of both, rather than imposing empty tasks and activities beyond their physical abilities. All children need real reasons for reading and writing and models of other people who are competent and confident readers and writers.

Assumption 4: Indoor, sedentary learning is more valuable than outdoor learning.

In spite of the implementation of the Foundation Stage curriculum, this assumption is very apparent in many settings. Adults often give strong messages by their presence, their comments, even their body language that indoors is best! In many settings, adults spend most of their time indoors, and see the outdoor area as a place for boys to let off steam. However, perceptive and experienced practitioners realise that the garden of their setting is prime learning space. They take every opportunity, whatever the weather, to be outside with the children, taking the whole curriculum out with them.

Assumption 5: Boys are noisier, louder and have no sensitivity; girls are quiet and have no capacity for adventure.

This is untrue. We know from research that boys have very strong feelings and sensitivity, but they learn very early that boys are not expected to show their feelings. From an early age boys are told to be brave, strong and to hide their feelings. Girls are sensitised in a different way, which encourages submission, safety and security.

Parents and practitioners expect boys to be noisy and lively - and boys live up to the expectations! They have more blood cells and about 30% more muscle bulk, so it is almost automatic for them to dominate the outdoor (and much indoor) play. Their behaviour models are other boys (and sometimes super-heroes) and their boisterous play is supported by their natural skills in experimenting and risk taking.

Research in classrooms in the United States has found that boys do in fact feel very deeply. They are much more affected by anxiety in others and feel the wrench of leaving their mothers <u>more</u> strongly than girls. They just learn from an early age to suppress their feelings of anxiety and loss.

Girls, on the other hand, follow the female models they see, staying indoors, close to adults and responding quietly in the ways which they know will gain approval. The assumptions that boys will be boys and girls will sit quietly continue to compound and reinforce behaviour, coming full circle to meet our assumptions and expectations.

Assumption 6: A content heavy curriculum suitable for older children (with an over-reliance on reading, writing and numeracy) can meet the needs of younger children.

We now have the Foundation Stage curriculum, with an emphasis on first hand experiences, play and talk. Everyone welcomes it and, well interpreted, it meets the needs of both boys and girls. However, the Foundation Profile is heavily weighted toward the things girls do well naturally and in doing so, could disadvantage boys. If this is so, boys (and some girls) are being disadvantaged at the first assessment hurdle, when personal and social development, communication and the beginnings of reading, writing and phonics outweigh interest and ability in investigation, technology, physical skills and creativity. The Foundation Stage Guidance encourages practitioners to provide for and support learning in all the six areas, to value the whole child, and to make learning relevant and vivid and real. The assessment of this curriculum emphasises some elements at the expense of others.

As practitioners, it is our job to challenge these assumptions and change the attitudes which result from them. We have a powerful influence in our settings, in our planning, in our contacts with parents and in our model for everyone.

Finding out about the differences and the similarities between boys and girls, enabling them to be the best they can, to challenge the stereotypes is a central purpose of the early years curriculum. This does not mean a rigid 'political correctness' or a soft 'anything goes' approach. It is a professional response to a professional job, and it requires us to read to research and above all to think about the individual children in our care, what makes them who they are and how we can support them in the most important stage of their lives.

Remember:
* Children develop 50% of their eventual ability to learn (sometimes described as their intelligence) before the age of four, and another 30% before they are eight.
* Adult interaction, adult models and adult support all make a massive difference to learning throughout childhood.
* Children watch us and take their messages from us on the value of who they are and what they do.

"Good outcomes for children are linked to adult-child interactions which involve 'sustained shared thinking' and open ended questioning"

EPPE Project, DfES

Existing assumptions - some questions

"A better world depends on making all groups happier and healthier. If we want more good men in the world, we must start treating boys with less blame and more understanding."
Raising Boys Steve Biddulph

? How can we clarify and (if necessary) challenge our assumptions about the behaviours and qualities of boys and girls?

? How do we encourage men to be part of our settings and of children's lives?

? How do we identify and celebrate the differences between boys and girls, and their individual strengths?

? How do we encourage all children to take part in all activities, despite the stereotypes present in their home lives or in the media?

? How do we help boys and girls to adopt the positive characteristics of both sexes?

? Do we sometimes fall into the trap of wishing that boys could be more like girls? What could we do about this?

? Do we value the girls who are strong and the boys who are sensitive?

? Do we ever use negative terms to describe children who don't meet stereotypical expectations? Do we ever say 'He's a Mummy's boy,' 'She's a real tomboy,' 'Come on, big boys don't cry,' 'I need a strong boy to help me.'? Do we challenge this type of language when we hear it?

? Do we have 'no go' areas for boys or girls play? Have we done anything to encourage or discourage this response?

? How can we make sure that children can be themselves, play the games and do the things they are comfortable with?

? Are the books, pictures and other images in the setting checked regularly to ensure that stereotypes of male and female roles are balanced with positive images of strong females and caring males?

? Do you ever encourage children to discuss the images of boys and girls they see in the media?

Tips for girls

"It is by expanding our understanding of male-female difference that we can show all children the vast potential of their lives in the educational world." *Boys and Girls learn Differently* Michael Gurian

- Talk with girls about the images they see on TV and in film. Discuss the ways these girls behave and if they think girls are really like this.

- Praise and notice girls more than you think you need to. They often miss out.

- Make sure you have plenty of books and pictures of females in strong positions, girls who are heroines, and characters who are brave and lead the action.

- Make sure role play areas don't have stereotypical clothing or objects - nurses' uniforms for girls, doctors' coats for the boys. Girls can be the mechanics, firemen and car wash operators, as well as acting out the traditional caring roles.

Tips for boys

- Tell stories and show pictures where boys are portrayed as strong <u>and</u> caring, and where mixed groups of children share exciting adventures together.

- Talk about the 'softer' side of superheroes and sportsmen. Collect pictures of them in caring activities, for example footballers with their children.

- Encourage boys to play in mixed groups, where children of both sexes and all gender types can join in.

- Notice, comment on and praise boys when they show kindness and care for others.

- Make sure you value the things boys do well, their willingness to have a go, to experiment, to be strong and active.

- Make sure role play areas don't give stereotypical messages - domestic play areas often only have female clothing, which limits boys' options.

Wider issues for all children

"Changing a child's mind is one thing, but changing my own is another. .. That girls and boys brains are different came as no surprise to the kids, who are living the differences every day. It was me who was surprised. How humbling that was. The kids knew more than I did."

Rose Aldrich, teacher quoted in *Boys and Girls learn Differently*

- Try to notice girls as much as you notice boys. Catch them all being good and getting it right, but don't only praise the behaviour that girls find easy.

- Gently challenge children's stereotyped views. Ask them what they think girls and boys are good at. Give them examples of female sportswomen or engineers and male chefs or ballet dancers.

- Check your own assumptions and stereotypes of children's behaviour, and challenge your own and colleagues' views.

- Check children's participation in activities. Make sure you don't have 'no go' areas for boys or girls. Adults (specially females) need to be present frequently in any areas seen as 'boys' areas'. Join in and provide a model.

"Perhaps it's best now to develop a new assumption, supported by brain based research: in a society that understands its children, we find that both boys and girls suffer privations and disadvantages owing, to a great extent to their brain systems' advantages and disadvantages in learning. This assumption would have been hard to accept twenty or thirty years ago, because gender bias was so flagrant against girls in schools. But now we must move on from old models and see what is really happening, not from political correctness, but from the inside out, through the lens of the brain."

Boys and Girls Learn Differently Michael Gurian

Physical development - key features

"By age six, teachers should expect a four-year span in maturation among students of the same chronological age."

Your Child's Growing Mind Jane Healey

It is blatantly obvious to anyone working in an early year's setting that, in general, physical development happens differently in boys and girls. A cursory glance around the outside area will reveal the un-surprising fact that most of the children tearing round on wheeled toys or catapulting themselves across the climbing frame....are boys!

It is also interesting to watch any early year's practitioner conducting an adult initiated activity, and story time is a classic example. The girls may be talkative and excitable, but when they are called upon to pay attention, they find it easier to calm down and concentrate. They can usually focus for longer periods of time and they are generally less easily distracted.

Once the story has begun, you can usually observe distinct differences in the way the children respond. Unless the story is very gripping, it is not unusual to see one or two of them wriggling about uncomfortably, pulling at a stray thread in their jumper or tugging at the Velcro on their shoes, and surprise, surprise, these children more often than not will be boys! The odds are stacked against them. Both developmental and biological differences make the whole business of sitting and listening more difficult for them than for the girls. They are behaving in a way that is very natural, and very understandable for young boys, but it is often difficult not to be annoyed by it. It's not their fault that they are often required to do things for which they are neither physiologically or developmentally ready, but this doesn't make things easy for the practitioner, especially in a climate where she is asked to achieve narrow, measurable targets in a short space of time. In a culture where downward pressure can be very real, her patience can be severely tested.

For many years, some very obvious differences have been overlooked. Here are some.

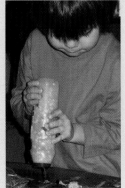

Testosterone

At the age of four, for reasons that nobody really understands, boys receive a sudden and huge surge of testosterone, causing a growth spurt and energetic and vigorous behaviour. They seem to have boundless energy and their play is full of action and adventure.

Physical development - key features

"(A girl) should spend plenty of time outdoors, playing and running around, to develop her strength, co-ordination and long-term health." *Raising Confident Girls* Elizabeth Hartley Brewer

Testosterone helps to build muscle - on average boys have 30 percent more muscle bulk than girls; making them stronger. It can also affect mood and lead to a boy becoming argumentative and restless. In general, it also makes boys more competitive than girls. Whether these differences exist because a 'boy brain' has a different type of hardwiring from a 'girl brain,' or whether they are cultural, nobody seems entirely sure.

It would seem that evolution has a lot to answer for! In hunter-gatherer societies the men were the hunters, and hunting is an activity requiring focus, speed, energy and strength.

So did males develop in this way out of necessity, or would they have been naturally stronger anyway? (Experiments on rats show that when female rats are injected with testosterone they attempt to fight and mate with each other). Testosterone injections can also help a feeble monkey climb to the top of the pecking order. At the end of the day it's a bit like the chicken and the egg, but for our purposes, it's all rather academic. What matters is how we cope with the differences.

Gross and fine motor control

While the boys are outside tearing around, they are developing excellent gross motor control, but their fine motor skills will not be nearly so well developed, making it difficult for them to handle pencils and scissors and deal with things like letter formation. They are still in the gross-motor development stage, and left to their own devices will want to move energetically for most of the time. Sitting still for any length of time

will be hard. Stillness is actually the most difficult of all movements to execute, calling for a huge amount of coordination and control.

Boys not only have higher activity levels, they also have lower levels of impulse control, making them doubly disadvantaged in a formal teaching situation. It's interesting to note that although some girls do have lots of energy and enthusiasm, they find it easier to control and manage that energy. For many boys, their muscles will actually be receiving messages to move, and whilst this is usually possible during periods of child-initiated learning it can cause difficulties in adult led situations.

Physical development

Impulse control

Boys need plenty of rough and tumble play, and it is this very play that teaches them important lessons. In rough and tumble play they learn self-control; they learn there is a point at which you stop, and it is much easier for a boy to learn this lesson when he has a strong male role model, and there aren't too many of these in early years settings.

In a predominantly female orientated environment, most boys will find that they are being urged to 'calm down' way before they want to. Boys are action-orientated and find some of the constraints imposed upon them in early education extremely difficult to endure.

Most boys struggle to meet the academic and developmental expectations placed upon them, and frequently find themselves penalised for simply behaving in ways that are natural for them. With their higher levels of impulse control, in a culture that begins formal learning so early, things are easier for girls. They find it easier to conform to the rules of the classroom. However, if an early years team is prepared to give this issue time and attention, the negative aspects of this situation can be minimised. When the adults in the setting have a genuine grasp of the fundamental differences in the physical development of boys and girls they can implement strategies that will really help boys to cope with the challenging situations they sometimes find themselves in.

"Girls do not generally need to move around as much while learning. Movement seems to help boys not only stimulate their brains, but also manage and relieve impulsive behaviour. Movement is also natural to boys in a closed space, thanks to their lower serotonin and higher metabolism, which creates fidgeting behaviour."

Boys and Girls Learn Differently Michael Gurian

Physical development - some questions

? If the odds are stacked against boys, how do we compensate without leaving the girls disadvantaged?

? How do we encourage girls to join in with physical and 'rough and tumble' activities?

? How do we recognise the difference between boys and girls in ability to calm down and concentrate? Do we always recognise children's efforts to do this?

? How can we offer boys (and some girls) the breaks they need in concentration during longer, whole group sessions?

? Stillness is a difficult task for all children, but most girls learn to do it before most boys. How can we encourage this to develop?

? Can we plan for or group children in activities to make allowances for differences in physical maturity?

? How can we help parents and children to understand what is going on during the testosterone surge? What are the useful strategies for dealing with the effects of this restlessness and aggression?

? How can we encourage girls to be more assertive and healthily competitive?

? How can we harness and engage the additional strength and energy of young boys?

? How can we provide opportunities for boys (and some girls) to develop fine motor skills in activities which have relevance for them?

? Is it possible to 'teach' impulse control? If so, how might we do it? And how do we recognise the feature in girls without making boys feel even less capable?

? We need more men in our settings - how could we provide these models?

? How could you find out whether in your setting you are penalising boys for their natural behaviour?

Tips for boys

"Girls, I notice, can still maximise their potential in a more sedentary, language orientated environment. My boys seem to grow best when they are active and setting up their own challenges."   Teacher quoted in *Boys and Girls learn Differently*

- Generally speaking, boys are stronger and more muscular than girls, so teach them how to solve problems without hitting or hurting each other.

- Boys tend to have a lower locus of control than girls, so help them to see the importance of thinking before they act. Talk with them about alternatives for solving problems.

- Provide lots of space and allow time for exercise and movement.

- Provide soft play areas for rough and tumble play.

- Make sure there are lots of opportunities for joining things together and taking things apart. Doing this will help boys develop the fine motor skills necessary for writing.

- Provide opportunities for woodwork, and an area where children can use screwdrivers to disassemble old, unwanted household objects, for example, radios and vacuum cleaners. N.B. Check to make sure that they do not contain any harmful components.

Tips for girls

- Encourage girls to participate in physical activities generally more associated with boys, for example, football and construction.

- Help girls to be more assertive when boys attempt to dominate space or resources.

- Provide ongoing access to the outside environment. Given the chance, children will naturally intersperse large and small physical movements and when outdoor play is constantly available it ceases to be the domain of domineering boys.

- Monitor physical activities to make sure that girls are not being marginalised by boys. If they are, discuss this with the children, generate possible solutions and provide follow up support.

Wider issues for all children

- Provide an outside area where there is plenty of challenge and opportunities for children to develop their large muscles.

- Plan activities that enable children to develop physical control through large-scale movement such as balancing, climbing, marching and moving to music.

- Help children to develop manipulative skills through using tools, cooking utensils, brushes, and scissors, etc.

- Check that your teaching style is active and multi-sensory. Young children like lots of action.

Cognitive (intellectual) development

"Pioneering studies also show that the IQs of children born in poverty, or of those who were premature at birth, can be significantly raised by exposure to toys, words, proper parenting and other stimuli."
Inside the Brain Ronald Kotulak

This child is seeing the bug on his hand, watching how it moves, learning how to handle it, in a way quite different from adults or even adolescents. He is building his brain, linking cells that have never been in touch with each other before and shaping his brain for the rest of his life. His care in handling a small creature is involving the use of both sides of his brain, so his hands, fingers, eyes can work together. And of course, he is outside. The natural environment for young children is the garden; perhaps we have forgotten this in our ever more sedentary and indoor lives.

The garden, with its multisensory, often unexpected events and objects, provides just the stimulation that children need to develop physically. But a garden also offers a unique situation for cognitive development. The growth of thinking, understanding and real knowledge come from deep immersion in experiences. Cognitive development does not come from being told, shown or demonstrated to. It comes from feeling, seeing, touching, smelling, tasting, preferably using the whole body as well as all the senses. It comes from practice, repetition and reinforcement, and from application of skills and emerging knowledge in different situations, and in the company of different people.

Why do babies and many young children put everything in their mouths? Babies are miniature scientists. They explore, find out about and test new objects by touching, tasting, smelling, banging, dropping, biting and every other means in their power! This is the way they make sense of the world, learning about things, beginning to understand how they work, and making links in their brains which will last them a lifetime. If babies are prevented from exploring the world around them their learning is limited, their physical development is damaged or delayed and their self esteem and will to learn can be destroyed. In order to become learners, children must be free to develop their bodies, their minds and their voices in the ways that come naturally to them, and what better place to do this than in a garden?

The more time children spend outside, exploring the world at their own pace and with all their senses, the more links they will make in their brains.

Cognitive development

"Even before birth, each child has the greatest mind that has ever existed, each child is the most powerful learning machine in the universe. Every young child has the potential, the instinct and the ability to learn."

How Babies Think Gopnik et al.

As children become more mobile, and more knowlegeable about the world, they begin to explore wider concepts - up/down; inside/outside; on/off; over here/over there. They begin to discover that they can affect the world around them, transporting things, wrapping things, climbing things. These activities,

often called schemas, are an important way in which younger children learn. We have all observed children who make the same model or read the same book over and over again, go up the ladder and down the slide time after time, get obsessed with putting things in bags and carrying them around, obsessively build walls, enclosures and dens, organise books, cars and other toys in careful patterns of colour or size. These children are making sense of their world, they are learning how to think, organise and understand their experiences.

Our job as practitioners is not just to provide for and watch this process, but to be part of it, to accompany children on their learning journey, supporting, enabling, enhancing their experiences. We need to know when to stand back, when to provide additional support or extension, when to ask questions, when to play alongside. The EPPE Report (Effective Practice in Pre-school Provision) has identified 'sustained shared thinking as one of the most powerful ways to help children's cognitive development. The sensitive company of an experienced adult or child can bring the inside thinking alive in words, enabling children to talk about their experiences and activities, and particularly to discuss what they are thinking. This process (called metacognition: thinking about thinking) is vital to understanding, and needs supportive discussions with open ended questions and spaces in the conversation for children to think about and verbalise their own thoughts and feelings.

Children also need plenty of uninterrupted time to practice and test out their newly evolved theories and emerging knowledge, and they do this through play and self initiated learning. Giving them genuine choices of where, what and who to play with ensures that they have time to continue their experiments and reinforce the pathways in their brains. Without this time to lay down and reinforce the physical patterning of their brains, children's cognitive development will be partial and fleeting, much like the theory we learn just for an exam.

Cognitive development

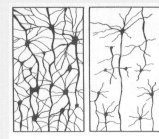

neural pathways in a **stimulated** brain

neural pathways in an **un-stimulated** brain

Building the brain for learning

Every baby is born with a hundred thousand million brain cells, and some are already joined to each other. In earlier sections we explored the difference in brain growth between boys and girls, and scientists now know that boy babies and girl babies have about the same number of linked cells in their brains at birth. However, boys have most of their linked cells in the separate halves of the brains (with more in the right half), while girls have started to link the two halves of the brain through the *corpus callosum,* the thick cord of connections between the two halves of the brain.

If a baby finds itself in a stimulating environment, full of people who are interested in them, have time for them and join them in their exploration of the world, they will continue to make learning links which physically change the structure of their brain. The brain on the left in the diagram above shows what happens. The links get thicker and stronger through play, practice and reinforcement, and if this play is active, exploratory and involves all the senses, the links will become stronger still. As children practice and revisit activities, a protective coating of a fatty substance called *myelin* builds up on their neural pathways, making the links stronger and faster.

And of course, if children have a healthy diet, plenty of water and sufficient rest, the coating will be stronger still. Stress, hunger, tiredness, additives and dehydration all erode myelin, leaving the neural pathways exposed to damage, so remember -

wet and well nourished brains work better!

"Exhaustion, anxiety, pressure or fear may make it impossible for neurons to send or receive the desired signals. Experts are concerned that well-intentioned parents may unwittingly short-circuit the pathways to skill development by forced learning."

Your Child's Growing Mind Jane Healey

Cognitive development - some gender differences

Recent research is also telling us that as children practice and reinforce their experiences, the differences between the brains of boys and girls influence how and what they learn.

<table>
<tr><th>Boys...</th><th>Girls...</th></tr>
<tr><td>

* usually start from general principles and apply these to individual circumstances, often through experiment. This is called deductive thinking or reasoning, and boys can do it faster than girls.
* usually find it easier than girls to think in abstracts and symbols, for instance in mathematical calculations. This is called abstract reasoning. The male brain likes conundrums, abstract debate and argument.
* often work silently, using few words as they work. When using words for their learning they are much more likely to develop codes or use jargon to communicate.
* tend to hear less and want more repetition and explanation They like logic and clarity in instruction and learning.
* get bored more easily than girls and need more stimulus to keep them involved. They are more likely to become disruptive when bored.
* use more space as they learn and play, both indoors and outside.
* really seem to be helped by movement, both during learning and in helping them to self manage impulsive behaviour.
* are less sensitive to group dynamics and social interaction, finding cooperative learning hard.

</td><td>

* usually start with concrete examples, building general theory from these examples. This is called Inductive reasoning, and girls can do it faster and earlier than boys.
* usually find it easier to use objects to work out calculations or mathematical problems. This is called concrete reasoning. Female brains find abstraction harder, preferring to use concrete examples.
* produce more words, speak earlier and use language as they learn. their leaning towards concrete reasoning means they prefer down to earth language and examples.
* girls are generally better listeners and can absorb much more detail in a discussion, instruction or conversation.
* are better at self-managing boredom! This means they are less likely to become disruptive;
* are able to work and play more 'neatly' using less space and invading others' space less.
* find it easier to sit still, need to move less and self-regulate more readily.
* find cooperative and collaborative learning easier, master it earlier and enjoy working in groups and talking together about what they are doing. This helps girls' learning.

</td></tr>
</table>

So what does this knowledge mean for our practice in working with both boys and girls?

Tips for boys

"Cognitive (or intellectual) development is development of the mind - the part of the brain that is used for recognising, reasoning, knowing and understanding."

Child Development, an Illustrated Guide Carolyn Meggitt and Gerald Sutherland

- Remember that boys have a lower 'boredom threshold'. Give them frequent brain breaks and opportunities for movement.
- Use simple, clear instructions (preferably one at a time) and don't get irritated by their need for a repeat or two!
- Generally speaking, boys are stronger and more muscular than girls, so teach them how to solve problems without hitting or hurting each other.
- Remember, boys need to move more, so try to take as much learning outside as possible.
- Plan for the fact that boys need more space for learning, indoors and outside.
- Praise and recognise boys' abilities to think in the abstract and work in mental mode.
- Help boys to work in groups by sensitive support.

Tips for girls

- Recognise girls' need for concrete objects, apparatus and examples in their learning.
- Recognise girls' abilities to listen and absorb detail from instructions and conversations.
- Offer plenty of opportunities for girls to work together collaboratively and cooperatively.
- Remember, most girls like (and need) to talk through their learning. Support this by helping them to recognise the difference between 'on task talk' and general gossip.
- Encourage girls to think inside their heads and develop mental and abstract strategies by talking about the different ways of working things out and thinking about them.

Wider issues for all children

"One of the simplest ways to to raise intelligence is to talk. Parents or other caregivers who talk a lot to infants during their first three years of life not only help them build better vocabularies, they also help them do something far more significant - raise their IQ level."   *Inside the Brain* Ronald Kotulak

- Provide and support active learning, both indoors and outside, by setting up a stimulating room and a garden full of experiences for all the senses.

- Give children plenty of time to practice their emerging skills and reinforce their growing knowledge through active, self initiated play.

- Notice and praise the learning skills of boys and girls, by emphasising that learning styles are not better or worse, just different.

- Talk about and share the different ways children are learning, by getting them to 'think about thinking'.

- Remember that each child is different and each child has already had a unique set of experiences, some of which happened before birth.

- Plan and support cooperative and collaborative activities for all children, but remember this may be difficult for most boys and some girls.

- A wet, well nourished, well rested and stress free body will support the development of a powerful brain.

"Good outcomes for children are linked to adult-child interactions which involve 'sustained shared thinking' and open ended questioning."

EPPE Project, DfES

Concentration and motivation

"In order for the brain not to be overwhelmed by the constant deluge of sensory input, some sort of filtering system must enable us to pay attention to what our bodymind deems the most important pieces of information and to ignore others."

Candace Pert, quoted by Alistair Smith in *The Brain's Behind It*

Wanting to learn, wanting to join in, wanting to listen - behaviours we expect of all children and take for granted in many. Of course, we all know that most children under seven are well motivated, want to come to nursery or school, and want to join in when they get there. But in order to understand motivation, we need to understand how it is 'switched on' and more importantly, how it sometimes gets 'switched off'. Motivation is closely linked with emotion. If we care about something, we will take notice of it and concentrate on it. Watch a baby gazing at its mother's face, a toddler spending long periods working out how to reach the latest 'object of desire', a four year old asking for the same story over and over again, a pre-teenager watching an older child. These children have an emotional relationship with the object or person they are watching, and this heightens their attention and the motivation to learn about it.

When we meet something new, we have a choice of how to react. We can react immediately as a reflex (in primitive 'fright or flight' mode); children sometimes hide or run away from something or someone new. Or we can react in a more measured way, analysing and watching the new thing, matching it against things we already know, assessing its threat or promise in a reflective way. The first sort of response is an emotional one, and emotion triggers physical motion towards or away from the experience; the second takes time and involvement.

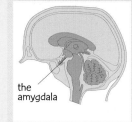

the amygdala

The amygdala, a small almond shaped part of the brain, about the size of your thumbnail, has a dramatic effect on how you respond. The amygdala regulates many functions (arousal and sleep, movement, reproduction, memory), and particularly feelings of fear, anxiety worry and aggression. It is also directly involved in the often subconscious decision about whether to use the reflexive or reflective response to new situations. To open the mind or to shut it down.

"Motivation has been described as a process that ties emotion to action."

The Brain's Behind It Alistair Smith

Concentration and motivation

"I am convinced that all children are motivated until we convince them otherwise."

Your Child's Growing Mind Jane M Healey

There appear to be three strands to a decision to attend to and react to a new situation or stimulus.

Firstly, the brain needs to be emotionally connected to the experience (and positive emotions, links and memories of similar events are obviously more likely to keep our attention locked in).

The second factor is challenge. We need to feel that the new experience has something to add to what we know. Interest and motivation are attracted to appropriate challenge.

The third factor is reward or payoff. This reward can be <u>external</u> - a smile, a sticker, a sweet, a treat; or <u>intrinsic</u> - internal satisfaction for doing something well. Intrinsic rewards will have a more lasting effect on our brains and our learning.

Jane Healey says:

'When adults start to take too much control, choose the challenges, and force them on children who aren't ready or able to achieve the personal payoff, trouble starts.'

We must take this advice very seriously in our work with young children. Research results are now clear: motivation is such an instinctive feature, one which we can switch OFF so easily, and once off, is very difficult to switch on again. Early experience of failure, ridicule, boredom, low challenge and external rewards build emotional circuits in the brain which trigger 'threat' responses, shutting down the brain and blanking out the new experience. And this response may last a lifetime!

Motivation for young children comes through success, enjoyment, and appropriate challenge. These result in new learning or reinforcement of existing brain patterns, laying down stronger myelin deposits which protect brain links. Success brings the reward of an open brain which responds to new experiences with interest, excitement and concentration, all of which expand understanding.

Think of the children you know. How well do they react to new learning challenges. How has their experience of life affected the way they learn?

Concentration and motivation

"In two of the schools that were operating an integrated, play-based approach, teachers said that this enabled children of all abilities to succeed: 'they can work at their own level and there will always be opportunities for them to be working at a level that is academically appropriate."   *A Study of Transition from the Foundation Stage to Key Stage 1* NFER

The message for all practitioners is clear. Children learn more and engage in the learning process if the three triggers are present: emotional connection, challenge and payoff.

Practitioners who understand the importance of these triggers make sure the way they plan, the way they organise their setting, the way they arrange resources, the way they involve children in their own learning, the way they value children's independence all demonstrate their commitment to engaging children. Some of the features of such settings are:

* flexible planning so children's arising interests can be incorporated;
* encouragement for independence and autonomy;
* plenty of child initiated learning at prime times of the day;
* long periods of time when children can continue the activities they become absorbed in;
* places for storing unfinished or ongoing projects;
* time for children to talk with each other and adults, before they work, during the activities and after they have finished;
* choice (for at least part of the day, and ideally a third of the day) when children can choose where, what and who they play with;
* easy access to resources and equipment, so children can find the things they need;
* flexible use of the indoor and outdoor environments for learning;
* a stimulating environment which results in challenging, enjoyable activities where external rewards are unnecessary because children are involved in and enjoying their work;
* an atmosphere where challenge is appropriate to the children's needs and abilities, and where success is noticed and rewarded appropriately.

In these settings motivation is secure, children's brains are stimulated and both boys and girls can experience success and reward for the activities they naturally enjoy and become engaged in.

Concentration and motivation - some questions

"Boys get bored more easily than girls; this quite often requires more and varying stimulants to keep them attentive. Girls are better at self-managing boredom during instructions and all aspects of education. This has a profound effect on all aspects of learning. Once the child has become bored, he is more likely to give up on learning but also to act out in such a way that class is disrupted and he is labelled a behavioural problem."   *Boys and Girls Learn Differently* Michael Gurian

? We know that boys and girls are interested in and motivated by different things. How do we use this knowledge in planning for learning?

? Girls seem to be able to manage boredom. How can we make sure girls don't just <u>appear</u> to be engaged in the things we expect them to do?

? If boys are less able to sustain interest when they are bored, what do we do to prevent their behaviour becoming disruptive?

? How do we provide appropriate challenge and motivating rewards?

? How do we ensure that the activities which stimulate boys' learning are recognised by a female dominated profession?

? When children move into Year 1, how do we support their teachers in maintaining the motivation of all children?

? The brain responds better to intrinsic rewards. How can we make sure children get positive feedback without over-emphasis on extrinsic rewards?

? How do we ensure that children have sufficient uninterrupted time to work on the activities which are important to them?

? In a busy, crowded setting, how do we make space for children's unfinished or continuing projects?

? Finding time for discussion, and joining children in their play will improve motivation, learning and language. How do you manage this?

? How can we check children's perceptions of our thinking? How interested are we in the things that interest them?

Tips for girls

- Watch girls carefully to check they are really engaged in what they are doing.
- Recognise the need for time to complete things. Girls may be willing to stop when we say so, because they are naturally more keen to please adults.
- Give girls time to talk to other children and adults. Talking helps girls with understanding more than it helps boys,
- Girls may well stand back and let boys overrun certain activities. Make sure girls get a fair share of all activities.
- Encourage girls to embark on physical challenges as well as the more sedentary activities.

Tips for boys

- Remember that boys are motivated by different things. Watch them and expand your knowledge of the activities, objects and places that 'switch on' boys.
- Remember that boys will be more likely to become engaged if they have access to the outdoors.
- Boys need frequent brain breaks when they are following our agenda or adult directed activities. Make sure you provide these.
- Plan plenty of time for boys to get actively involved in projects and challenges.
- Be flexible about the places, positions and situations where boys choose to work and play. Use this knowledge when you are directing the tasks.

Wider issues for all children

"Girls learn while attending to a code of social interaction better than boys do. Boys tend to focus on performing the task well, without so much sensitivity to the emotions of others around them. However, 'pecking orders' are flagrantly important to boys, and they are often fragile learners when they are low in the pecking order."

Boys and Girls Learn Differently Michael Gurian

- **Provide** places where unfinished or ongoing projects can be safely left. **This may be difficult in a small setting, but very stimulating for concentration and persistence.**

- Plan flexibly, **so children can follow their interests for long periods of time and set their own challenges.**

- Make sure you organise your setting so children can be as independent and autonomous as possible.

- Know your children well, **so you don't underestimate their ability to manage their own learning and set their own challenges.**

- Remember that intrinsic rewards are more powerful then extrinsic rewards. **Children who are really engaged, challenged and motivated in their work and play are found not to need or want rewards. The interest of others and the enjoyment of learning are enough.**

"I don't choose the building or Lego any more. Always, just when I get to finishing a model, it's time to clear up and she says I have to put it back in the box. I never get time to play with it."

a boy in a Foundation Stage setting

Language development

"... the language part of the brain is not fully formed until about the age of thirteen."

Raising Boys Steve Biddulph

It is now widely accepted that there are distinct differences in the ways that boys and girls acquire and use language. At an early age girls are more able to articulate words and have more extensive vocabularies than boys. They show more expertise in controlling the dynamics of language. In their speech they pause less, and the quality and length of their sentences is generally more complex. So why is this the case, and how do these differences impact on boys in early year's settings?

The two hemispheres of the brain

Broadly speaking, the left hemisphere of the brain deals with speech production and comprehension, while the right hemisphere processes visual patterns, music, emotions and spatial relationships. Scanning has shown that boys and girls access these centres differently. It is as if the anatomy of the brain is more supportive to girls, enabling them to have easier access to the language processing side of the brain.

The growing brain

In all human babies, the left side of the brain grows more slowly than the right, but it grows slower in males. Research has shown that hormones are largely responsible for this. Testosterone in a boy's bloodstream slows down the process, whereas oestrogen in a girl's blood actually stimulates the growth of brain cells. It is therefore extremely significant that at around four years of age boys receive a massive surge of testosterone!

At around the same time as boys start school, their brains are struggling to make the connections

required to cope with formal learning, and in our culture they simply don't have enough time. They find themselves asked to cope with processes for which their brains are not yet programmed. As the right brain is growing if tries to make connections with the left, but in boys, the left brain is not ready. As Steve Biddulph explains in Raising Boys,

'...the nerve cells reaching across from the right cannot find a place to plug in. So they go back to the right side where they came from and plug in there instead. As a result, the right half of a boy's brain is richer in internal connections but poorer in cross connections to the other half.'

Language development
Access to the two hemispheres of the brain... nature or nurture?

Imaging techniques can now be used to assess the area of the brain responsible for the processing of language. Recent research has shown that when males process language, electrical activity in the brain is almost exclusively based in the left hemisphere. By comparison, women activate centres in both the right and left hemispheres. MRI scans have made neural systems visible and helped us to understand that females not only analyse information using both hemispheres simultaneously, they can even transfer processing from one hemisphere to another. If a female has a processing difficulty in the left hemisphere, she can use other systems in the right. Males are unable to make this transfer, which could explain why males identified with dyslexia outnumber females 4 to1. In contrast, from the earliest age boys show better abilities in spatial tasks, and this is probably the result of evolution. Men had to manufacture tools and weapons and hunt for food, which required spatial abilities. Women gathered food and cared for the children, and consequently developed in different ways.

MRI scans also show that in females, two regions of the brain responsible for processing language are proportionately 20 to 30% larger than in males. As yet, no-one is sure whether this is biological or cultural; whether girls are born with this advantage, or whether they develop it through increased practice. Either way, we do know that where language learning is concerned there are distinct windows of opportunity between the years of zero and eight, and that conversation is a major way of stimulating the growing brain. Could it be that a boy's need for speed and action results in less time for talk?

The corpus callosum
We have already noted that the corpus callosum in boys is proportionately smaller in size and there are fewer connections running from one side to the other. While girl's brains are making connections across the corpus callosum, boy's brains are making more lateral connections. Until the age of four all children are predominately 'creatures of the right brain' but evidence suggests that girls then show increased levels of activity in the left brain and are more able to process information sequentially. This enables them to deal with letter recognition, word building and sentence formation. In boys, the transition between right and left hemisphere functioning does not take place until around six, or even later, placing them at a distinct disadvantage in UK schools today.

Language development

Language learning and hearing

There can be little doubt that in terms of literacy and perhaps all school based education, the most fundamental skill of all is listening. Unless children can discriminate between sounds and listen with growing attention, they will be slow to understand and slow to talk, and here boys can be at a disadvantage. Boys have growth spurts which can affect their ear canals and lead to significant temporary hearing loss. Often when we think they are not paying attention they actually haven't heard us. Hearing difficulties are more common in boys and 70 percent of boys of school age have poorer hearing than their female counterparts. This makes it difficult for them to hear sounds and syllables and segment and blend. It can also mean that they experience difficulties in reading and in following instructions. Some six year old children find it hard to understand sentences of more than eight words, so it is really important that practitioners use short sentences and check that children have understood before going on.

Bridging the gap

All in all, girls are programmed to process language more effectively than boys, and although boys catch up eventually, this may not happen if their disposition to learn has been damaged. Such damage can happen very easily in a culture that begins formal learning at an early age. In a system that makes few allowances for the fundamental differences between girls and boys, it is down to all early year's practitioners to do all they can to help boys with language processing.

"Research shows us that boys' brains are 'wired' in such a way that language is a more difficult skill for them to acquire and use effectively in learning than it is for girls. Thus in our early-childhood classes, most of my language activities are paired with movement and/or the use of manipulatives. This strategy seems to work especially well with young boys."

Kathi, a teacher quoted in *Boys and Girls Learn Differently*

Language development - some questions

"Language is the means by which the brain develops its ability to act as a control centre for thinking, learning and planning."

Your Child's Growing Mind Jane Healey

? We know there are differences in the ways boys and girls acquire and use language. How do we plan for this?

? If girls are more enthusiastic and fluent language users, do we make enough space and time for boys to contribute?

? Testosterone has a marked effect on young boys. How might this affect their confidence in experimenting with language, and how can we overcome this?

? If formal learning actually switches boys' brains off, how do we make the curriculum more active and practical, particularly as they get a bit older?

? The different ways girls and boys process language is fascinating. Does this have any messages for us as a mainly female profession?

? Boys are better at spatial tasks. What does this mean, and how can we ensure that we plan plenty of these to build boys' confidence and self esteem?

? Most boys (and some girls) are naturally 'speedy' and active. How do we make time for them to engage in conversations? Do these always need to be indoors on the carpet?

? Most girls find letter recognition, word building and sentence formation easy. How can we maintain the progress of girls while we wait and watch for the boys to be ready?

? Many young boys suffer temporary hearing loss. They may not be aware of this! How do we ensure that all children can hear what is going on?

? Most boys catch up eventually. How do we make sure that their self esteem and disposition to learn has not been damaged or even destroyed by too much formality too early?

? Which books, resources, spaces and activities interest and motivate boys to use and develop language? Do we offer these on a daily basis?

Tips for boys

"Girls tend to prefer to have things conceptualised in usable, everyday language, replete with concrete details. Boys often find jargon and coded language more interesting.... boys tend to work out codes among themselves and rely on coded language to communicate."

Boys and Girls Learn Differently Michael Gurian

- When setting tasks for boys, give clear, precise instructions.

- Give boys one task at a time. Multi-tasking really is easier for girls!

- Make time to talk with and read to boys. Saturate them with talk and stories.

- Tune in to the things that boys are interested in and make these things a focus for talk and activities.

- Remember that many boys have a preference for non-fiction, so make sure that there are plenty of quality non-fiction texts in your setting, and not just in the book corner.

- When talking with boys, be patient and take time.

- Boys love role-play and drama, so DO involve yourself in this kind of play and use it as a context for language development.

- Provide a range of prop boxes, and build literacy into the things boys are interested in.

Tips for girls

- Provide quiet areas away from more boisterous play where girls can engage in conversation.

- Provide plenty of telephones. The more you provide, the more they'll talk!

- Tune in to the things that the girls are interested in and use those things as a context for talk. Language is learned most effectively when it is interesting and relevant.

Wider issues for all children

"Parents who talk to their children the most tend to praise the children's accomplishments, respond to their questions, provide guidance rather than commands, and use many different words in a variety of combinations. This type of interaction can accurately predict the vocabulary growth, vocabulary use, and IQ scores of children." (the effect of this is still apparent at nine years old!)

Inside the Brain Ronald Kotulak

- Make speaking and listening a priority for all children.

- Listen carefully to children before you launch into conversation. Don't be afraid of silences and allow time for children to initiate conversations.

- Ensure that you don't ask too any questions. Ask quality questions and allow children time to answer.

- Be excited about what children have to say.

- Reduce your control. Observe and watch the children and become a real play-partner.

- Read the quote on this page. How can practitioners support these findings, both for children who spend much of their day in day-care, and those who do not?

"The richer the sensory environment and the greater our freedom to explore it, the more intricate will be the patterns for learning, thought and creativity."

Smart Moves Carla Hannaford

Emotional and social development

"Studies have shown that that parents hug and cuddle girl children far more, even as newborn babies."

Raising Boys Steve Biddulph

Boys, girls and relationships

Take a group of young girls, give them some construction equipment and observe what happens. Generally speaking, they will talk about what they are going to do and how they are going to do it. They will probably work collaboratively and they will be most likely to build a house, around which they will develop a narrative.

Now give that same equipment to a group of boys. What will follow will be very different. They will be most likely to grab equipment for themselves, there will be a lot less talk and they will probably work alone. Within a short space of time you will begin to hear phrases like, 'Mine's taller than yours.....bigger than yours.....faster than yours, etc.' It is interesting to note that when boys work together they tend to prefer to work side by side rather than face to face...a habit that persists into adulthood. (Go into any pub and you are likely to see groups of women conversing around tables, whereas the men are often happy standing at the bar...side by side!). Boys and girls relate differently to each other and they relate differently to adults.

Boys, girls and emotions

The emotional brain (amygdala) is situated in the limbic system, and here again there are significant differences between boys and girls. Current research has demonstrated that females, on average, have a larger deep limbic system than males. This gives females advantages from an emotional point of view. They find it generally easier to identify their feelings than men, and are better able to express those feelings. They also demonstrate an increased ability to bond and be connected to others.

All boys have feelings but it is not always easy for them to express what they feel. In the first place, boys' brains are hard wired in such a way that it is more difficult for them to take feelings and impressions from the right side of the brain. From early on, boy babies are less sensitive to faces. Girl babies spend more time actually focusing on faces, so they get a lot more practice in 'emotional referencing.' Girl babies also have a much better sense of touch.

Emotional and social development

When a boy experiences a feeling in the right side of his brain he can sometimes find it difficult to make the shift into the left hemisphere in order to find the words to express that feeling. Boys tend to be action-orientated, and are much more likely to respond physically to how they feel. They tend to have lower levels of impulse control and are much more inclined to act first without thinking things through.

Girls on the other hand tend to be more naturally disposed to spend time thinking things over. Given this scenario it seems even more imperative that we help boys <u>and</u> girls to recognise and talk about feelings, and find non-aggressive ways of resolving conflicts.

In the main it would probably be fair to say that boys show less emotion than girls, but from this we cannot conclude that they actually feel less. Some research studies which have looked at boys' reactions to distress in others indicate that they may actually feel more.

Other findings suggest that when boys become affected by emotions they may be less effective at managing those emotions. Researchers at the University of Arizona played a tape of a baby crying to a group of five and six year old boys and girls. Prior to the experiment an adult demonstrated how to calm the baby down by talking to it over an intercom. They then monitored the children's reactions. What ensued what very interesting. The girls were less upset by the crying than the boys. They made more attempts to calm the baby down and were less inclined to turn the speaker off. The boys were more likely to turn off the crying and more likely to act aggressively towards the baby. The researchers concluded that the boys were more easily stressed by emotional responses and may prefer to avoid them. Put bluntly, if boys have difficulty managing their own emotions, they are much more likely to be unresponsive to upset in others.

It is also interesting to note that if a mother withdraws her presence or her warmth in the early years, boys find this more difficult than girls; more difficult to control their pain, and consequently, shut down the part of them that connect with her.

"In kindergarten, boys are primarily interested in objects and things; girls are primarily interested in people and relationships."

Boys and Girls Learn Differently Michael Gurian

Stereotypical ideas about masculine toughness still make it difficult for a boy to feel at ease expressing feelings. Many boys learn at a very early age that being too open about expressing what they feel can get them labelled as 'sissies.' Consequently, they learn early on that they must hide both their feelings and their fears, and this can prove a real barrier to them developing a full range of emotional resources. Things are getting better, but in the main we still live in a culture that makes it easier for girls to develop emotionally.

Whatever we may like to think to the contrary, we live in a society where adults treat boys and girls differently. Studies have shown that girl babies tend to get cuddled far more than boy babies and that when a young child is smacked, adults will hit boys harder than girls. It may be completely unintentional, but we tend to discourage emotional awareness in boys. Mothers speak more about sadness and distress with girls than they do with boys. One study observing the talk of pre-school children found that

girls were six times more likely to use the word 'love' and twice as likely to use the word 'sad' as boys.

It is also interesting to note the way in which, when a girl is upset, adults are quick to offer comfort and support. By contrast, when a boy hurts himself or is upset, it is not uncommon to hear adults respond with, 'Come on, be a brave boy!' Understanding emotions is at the heart of all relationships, and if we want to improve the quality of relationships, it is essential that we pay close attention to the emotional education of both girls and boys.

"In the years between birth and six, boys need lots of affection so they can 'learn to love'. Talking and teaching one-to-one helps them connect to the world."

"Boys feel insecure and in danger if there isn't enough structure in a situation. If no-one is in charge, they begin jostling with each other to establish a pecking order."

Raising Boys Steve Biddulph

Emotional & social development - some questions

? Boys and girls work differently in groups. How do we plan for and respond to this?

? If boys are more comfortable working side by side, how does this affect our work in one-to-one and small groups?

? Most girls find it easier to talk about feelings than most boys. Which activities and resources might help boys to discuss their feelings and emotions?

? Most girls are better than boys at understanding faces and expressions. How can we help boys to be more aware of these?

? Boys are 'action oriented'. How do we help them to acquire the vocabulary to talk about their feelings and emotions?

? How can we help boys to develop the concept of 'think before you act' so they are not so impulsive when deep emotions are involved?

? Most boys (and some girls) are naturally 'speedy' and active. How do we make time for them to engage in conversations? Do these always need to be indoors on the carpet?

? Most girls spend some time thinking. How can we recognise this skill and talk about its benefits?

? Many boys may <u>feel</u> more emotion than most girls, even though they find it more difficult to express. How can we help them to express what they feel?

? How can we challenge the stereotypical ideas of the ways children should behave, while being sensitive to the differing expectations at home, in our settings, in society, on TV?

? How can we develop responses, both physical and verbal, which give support equally to all children? How can we use physical demonstrations of affection, support and praise, so all children understand their meaning and worth?

? How could you find out whether your responses to the boys and girls in your setting are affected by stereotypes?

Tips for girls

"Learning seems to occur best when positive emotions facilitate chemical secretions in the brain that help messages cross synapses. These substances, called neurotransmitters, may particularly help learning when the child is rested, in control, and secure. Exhaustion, anxiety, pressure, or fear may make it impossible for the neurons to send or receive the desired signals."

Your Child's Growing Mind Jane Healey

- Help girls to be assertive when the more boisterous behaviour of boys impacts upon their play.
- Help girls to explain their feelings and their needs when challenged by more forceful peers.
- Read and tell stories where female characters have equality within relationships. There are still many stories where female characters are more passive than males.

Tips for boys

- Be aware of the fact that boys can experience higher levels of separation anxiety than girls.
- Create an ethos and environment where there are clear structures and ground rules. This enables boys to feel secure.
- Monitor to ensure that you do not treat boys more harshly than girls.
- Ensure that you show boys as much affection as you show girls.
- Be patient and remember that language and expression are two specific weak areas for boys, making it harder for them to express their feelings.
- Praise boys and girls equally.
- Help boys to read faces and body language. (They find this more difficult than girls do)
- Make it OK to ask for help.

Broader issues for all children

"My concern is with a key set of these 'other characteristics'. Emotional intelligence: abilities such as being able to motivate oneself and persist in the face of frustrations; to control impulse and delay gratification; to regulate one's moods and keep distress from swamping the ability to think; to empathise and to hope."

Emotional Intelligence Daniel Goleman

- Read stories that enable all children, and boys in particular, to understand that it is alright to be frightened or upset.

- Plan activities that enable children to work in a variety of groupings, including mixed groups.

- Develop the children's 'emotional vocabulary,' and help them to recognise, acknowledge and name feelings in appropriate ways.

- Don't be afraid to talk about your own feelings. Remember that children learn by listening, watching and copying, so model positive relationships with your colleagues.

- Plan time to talk about relationships and encourage the children to talk about the people who are important to them.

- Make sure that your programme of work for PSED helps children to see the value of positive relationships and supports them in developing relationship skills.

"The emotional mind is far quicker than the rational mind, springing into action without pausing even a moment to consider what it is doing. Its quickness precludes the deliberate, analytical reflection that is the hallmark of the thinking mind."

Emotional Intelligence Daniel Goleman

Role models

"Role modelling is wired in as an evolutionary trait in humans. By watching a person we admire in action, our brain takes in a cluster of skills, attitudes and values."

Raising Boys Steve Biddulph

Early years settings are largely feminine environments where male staff are the exception rather than the rule, and this puts boys at a considerable disadvantage. In a setting where none of the adults are male, there is nobody with first hand experience of what it feels like to be a young boy in early education, and this has serious implications for practice.

Although an all female team may **think** that they are catering equally for the needs of both girls and boys, the reality may be quite different. As Vivian Gussin Paley points out in her book 'Boys and Girls: Superheroes in the Doll Corner';

'When the children separate by sex, I, the teacher, am more often on the girls' side. We move at the same pace and reach for the same activities, while the boys barricade themselves in the blocks, periodically making forays into female territory.'

Any female practitioner reading this honest statement cannot fail to question the extent to which she does the same thing, especially during periods of child-initiated learning. Could it be that as women we are unconsciously drawn to involving ourselves with the activities that are most popular with the girls, and could this mean, that by default, the boys' play is less well supported? Take, for example, fantasy play, which is extremely popular with most boys. Women often feel quite uncomfortable with this type of play. If we are honest, many of us would admit to being far happier in the graphics area than the block area, more motivated to engage with domestic play than superhero play, and perhaps happier to be inside rather than outside.

And what messages is this giving the boys? Could it be that inadvertently we are failing to value the things that are important to boys, and perhaps even diverting them from the things that really interest them? For any setting seriously committed to equality there may be conflicts to be faced. We need to be courageous; willing to be self-critical in a searching and positive way.

Role models

You need only to look at what happens when an adult male enters an early years setting where there are no male practitioners. The boys will flock around him like bees around a honey pot. It is as if know that this person can relate to something within them that their female practitioners cannot, and the truth is, they are probably right.

Home and community experiences

By the time a boy enters an early years setting he has already formed some strong ideas about what being male is all about. But in a mainly female environment he has no-one against whom to test his ideas. All he has to go on are the experiences of maleness encountered in the home and community, and this could present some boys with huge difficulties. They may come from a home or community where it is not seen as 'macho' to be involved in academic activities such as reading or writing. Equally, their experience of maleness may be associated with harshness or aggression, and without

 other male role models, how can they begin to build a broader picture of what being male is all about?

There may be considerable differences between what is expected of the child at home and what is expected in the setting, and never is this so apparent than in conflict situations. If a boy comes from a background where males deal with conflicts by force, he will not find it easy to understand why he cannot hit out in the setting. It is interesting to consider this dilemma in the context of superhero play. Superheroes have simple bold behaviours, strength and the power to fight off danger. This is very appealing to young boys (and some girls) who are going through the process of learning to be independent. Where there are male role models in an early years setting, boys can see first hand that not all males solve their problems by force.

There may be many young boys who only ever see the 'macho' side of maleness. If there are no male staff in the setting, they may never see a man in a caring role.

What about the girls?

In a mainly female environment, it may seem that things are rigged against the boys and that the girls have the advantage. However, there are inherent dangers for the girls also. The professionals they are spending their time with fulfil the archetypal female role. They are carers and nurturers. Generally speaking, they don't carry spanners, ride motor bikes or climb scaffolding, so girls whose home and community experiences also exclude such role models may form a narrow picture of what being female is all about. They may only associate being female with softness, passivity and compliance.

Parental perceptions

Young children arrive at their early years settings heavily influenced by their parent's experiences of school, and where these experiences have been negative they may well have a detrimental effect on their children. We know from the EPPE project that parents who actively engage in activities with their children promote valuable intellectual and social development. We also know that the home learning environment is only moderately associated with social class. What parents <u>do</u> is more important than <u>who they are</u>.

Where parents support the work of the early years setting children develop positive attitudes towards education, but for some parents, scarred by their own experiences of the educational system, giving their children this support may not be easy. As one father reported,
'I walk into a school building and I can feel my chest get tight. It's a place that's up to no good. I had a difficult time in school when I was a kid over stuff I had no control over. What I learned in school was that, in some essential ways that matter to other people, I didn't measure up.'

Such experiences are bound to impact and make it difficult for a person to support their child in forming positive attitudes towards education and learning.

"... children's play behaviour is not carved in stone and is amenable to sensitive practitioners, like sculptors, working with, rather than against the grain of children's play."

We Don't Play with Guns Here Penny Holland

Role models - some questions

? Early Years settings are largely staffed by women. Is there anything we should or could be doing to increase all children's contacts with men?

? How can practitioners find out whether they are REALLY catering equally for boys and girls?

? Most women are unconsciously drawn to activities generally enjoyed by girls. How can we ensure that the activities boys enjoy are recognised, valued and supported by adults?

? What message do we give to boys if the adults obviously avoid or under-value outdoor, messy and active play?

? What are the concepts of masculinity and femininity in the community around your setting? How do these concepts and expectations affect the children you work with?

? Should parents be involved in discussion about gender roles? If so, how could you involve them? What are the tensions around involving parents in these issues?

? What can you do when the children have violent or aggressive models of male behaviour at home? And how do you respond to simplistic views about the roles of girls and women?

? How can you use male visitors to improve the profile and acceptability of reading and writing?

? How can practitioners respond when children behave violently, copying what they have seen at home or in the community?

? Superhero play is common in young boys (and some girls). It is their way of 'trying on' independence and strength. How do you handle this in your setting? Does it work?

? Do you consider (and challenge) stereotypical views of women? Practitioners may find it difficult to to provide role models of strength, technical ability, bravery. How could you present these features to the girls and boys in your care?

? Some parents have negative views of education and the adults who work in it. How can you influence this view?

Tips for boys

- Wherever possible, invite men into your setting to talk and interact with the boys

- Take time to value the things that boys are interested in.

- Display images of men that are not stereotypical. For example, hairdresser, nurse, etc.

- Encourage boys to talk about the men they look up to as role models.

- Plan activities and experiences that enable boys to focus on gender. Talk with them about what it means to be a boy, and challenge any limiting beliefs.

Tips for girls

- Display images of girls and women in a wide range of roles. For example, engineer, footballer, mechanic, plumber, etc.

- Wherever possible, invite women who do unconventional jobs into your setting to share their experiences with the children.

- Check that the girls are not marginalised in certain areas of your provision, for example, block play.

- Talk with the girls about what it means to be a girl and challenge any limiting beliefs.

- Encourage girls to access the full range of provision.

Wider issues for all children

"Mothers provide a role model for their daughters, but they also provide their sons and daughters with many lessons on the nature of men. If children see a respectful, loving relationship and hear their mothers talking about their father and other men with affection and respect, they take on these attitudes. If their mother puts their father down the children may learn to despise their father in particular and men in general."

Bringing the Best Out in Boys Lucinda Neall

- Does the passage above have messages for practitioners too? What sort of role models do children in your setting see, hear and overhear?

- Be aware of your own perceptions of gender. Examine your behaviour. Do you unconsciously reinforce negative gender stereotypes?

- Sensitively challenge stereotypical thinking in children, colleagues, parents and carers and the wider community.

- Ensure that relevant gender issues are openly discussed in a positive way with all members of the early year's team.

- Ask questions that uncover stereotypical thinking.
  For example:
  Can boys have long hair? Can girls be footballers?

- Make the best possible use of puppets and persona dolls to explore gender related issues.

- Consciously become aware of where you spend your time during periods of child-initiated learning.

- Implement a monitoring programme to raise awareness of gender related issues.

Media influences

"It is important to remember that children are not responsible for the media diet they are offered. That responsibility is one that rests entirely in the adult world."

We Don't Play with Guns Here Penny Holland

Spend just a few minutes observing the play of young boys and the influence of the media on that play will be instantly apparent! Television, video and computer games now fill homes with daylong noise and powerful images that make a strong impression on the young viewer. Even pictures in magazines and catalogues lay down strong ideas about what being a boy is all about. On one page you can see the girls, smiling and friendly, often standing in groups. Then look at the 'boy' page, and you can see instantly that they have been told not to smile; to look at the camera with a stare that is lean, mean and hard. It would be unfair to suggest that all advertisers promote this kind of image of boys, but there is still plenty of this sort of stuff around.

For young boys in our settings, what they see on television and read about in comics has a massive impact. Each year there are new superheroes for them to imitate. We can see them flying around with coats worn only by the hood, shooting, kicking, hitting and chopping as they mimic the roles they have seen on television. They are exploring what it is like to be in control, and from the messages that they have picked up they know that it is the most powerful people who have the best gadgets and the most powerful weapons. They are constantly absorbing these messages about the world through television, computers, videos and books, and in recent years media coverage of major war zones has bought international conflict straight into our living rooms. There are very few young children who have not seen coverage of terrorists, criminals and suicide bombers.

Such images perpetuate the notion of the rough, tough, powerful man and do little to promote the idea of the caring nurturing side of being male. Play derived from media influences frequently involves violent, physical action and causes conflict and disruption, so it is only natural that it should be a cause of concern for early years practitioners.

Media influences

However, if we can understand the process that underpins such play and makes it so attractive to young children, especially boys, we can channel it productively and enable children to use play as a tool for thinking.

So, why are superheroes so attractive to young boys? Children are extremely interested in the way that their actions affect others. Their view of the world is constructed in terms of clear, simple concrete actions and physical characteristics, and this is the world of the superhero! With their simple, bold actions they can fight off danger and solve problems, something that is extremely appealing, especially to a young child. In short, superheroes are powerful. They are also usually attractive, strong and fast; characteristics that are also very appealing to young boys. So how can early year's practitioners respond to the young child's need for power and control?

Looking for alternatives

Superheroes may be great in the world of fantasy, but in reality they present a very unrealistic model of problem solving. The EPPE project has identified teaching conflict resolution as a characteristic of the best settings, and this is understandable as through this process children learn to solve problems through good assertive communication. They also develop sensitivity to the feelings of others as they learn to express their own emotions, thoughts and needs. They experience genuine power as they see the way in which others respond. Through effective conflict resolution we can meet children's developmental needs in an appropriate way, and at the same time enable them to learn a crucial life skill.

Every setting can benefit from looking at their policy for supporting children in resolving conflicts.

"Boys' stories are filled with excitement and action, ignoring the victims; girls' stories pay attention to human dynamics, with particular concern with victim's feelings."

Boys and Girls Learn Differently Michael Gurian

Dealing with gun play

Perhaps most worryingly, superheroes usually carry guns with which to 'zap' people, and this forces all settings to clarify their policy with regard to gun play. Some settings may choose to ban it completely while others will decide to manage it. This is a challenging issue for all of us, but at the end of the day we need to recognise what is going on behind the play. In the 21st century, many children actually live in a gun culture, and gun play enables them to explore the anxieties and issues about keeping safe and solving problems. Through gun play they are exploring what it feels like to have a gun or to not have a gun. They are exploring relationships and ways of keeping safe, and if we suppress this play, we suppress their thinking and throw away a valuable opportunity to influence that thinking.

Gun play also fulfils the young boys need to dash around in a noisy boisterous way, and if we can involve ourselves in that play we can model ethical responses to difficult moral dilemmas. It is understandable that we may want to take the approach that 'guns are wrong because they kill people,' and some practitioners may have very strong opinions about this issue, but when we stop children from playing out the things that are on their minds, there are serious consequences.

In the first place, the children will simply take the play underground. Perhaps more importantly they will get a very strong message that what they know about, are perhaps worried about, and are interested to know more about, is not valued by their practitioners. As one disappointed five year old boy remarked at the end of his first day at school, 'You can't do anything!' The trouble wasn't really that he couldn't do anything, of course, but that everything he loved to do - run, throw, wrestle, climb - was outlawed in the classroom. Many of the things in which boys are interested are marginalised in their settings, and this simply builds on the idea that education is not relevant. A wise setting not only recognises this but uses this interest to promote the skills of thinking, communicating and negotiating.

"Many practitioners do not value war, weapon and superhero play as a form of imaginative play. Many feel that its themes are simply dictated by films, video and TV series, which have limited and repetetive contents based crudely on a struggle between good and evil and thus offer chidlren little in terms of extended maginative play ..... A major difficulty with this analysis is that because chidlren are generally interrupted in such play scenarios I do not feel we can begin to evaluate the imaginative potential of such scenarios unless we allow them to develop." *We Don't Play with Guns Here* Penny Holland

Media influences - some questions

? We cannot ignore the influences of the media. How should we respond?

? Both boys and girls are affected by media influences. Are we aware of the ways this happens and the different messages being received?

? Look at some magazines and catalogues. How are the boys and the girls behaving? Is there a difference? What are they playing with? How many caring males can you find? How many strong and independent females?

? Watch a bit of Saturday morning TV (if you have time!). What are the programmes and the adverts saying to impressionable young children? What are the gender views, specially in the advertisements?

? What are the messages about gadgets, 'designer gear', footwear, etc. in the media? How do these affect children? What can we do to counteract these messages?

? Does our behaviour encourage, contradict or confuse young children?

? How has your setting responded to the increasing media coverage of wars, disasters, terrorism, violence? Do you feel confident of your feelings and how to respond?

? Superhero play is common among most young boys and some young girls. Do you understand why children need to respond in this way? Have you discussed how to handle superhero play in your setting?

? What is conflict resolution, and how can we teach it to children?

? How do we help children to understand the difference between assertive and aggressive behaviour and language?

? How should we respond to gun play? Join it? Ban it? Try to suppress it? Have you discussed this in your setting? Have you an agreed response?

Tips for girls

Girls have "...a triple dose of expectation: to be emotionally successful, to be emotionally independent and to achieve the heightened standard of beauty that cosmetics, clothes, etc. can now provide."

Raising Confident Girls Elizabeth Hartley-Brewer

- Talk with the girls about their media influences. Be interested and use their ideas as a catalyst for experiences in role-play and creative work.

- Talk with the girls about your own media influences. Include women who present an alternative to 'princess or Cinderella roles.'

- Encourage girls to be assertive when gun play and superhero play conflict with other forms of play.

- Openly support discussion around conflict situations.

- Provide costumes and props that relate to a range of media influences, not just the stereotypical female roles.

Tips for boys

- Value the characters and personalities that influence the boys.

- Don't stifle their play with disapproval. Rather, discuss alternative ways of doing things.

- The people who influence boys are frequently powerful, so help them to explore the negative and positive implications of power.

- Take time to understand the ways in which boys use superhero play as a means of exploring concepts of power and control.

- Provide ways for boys to use their strength safely, and channel their drive and energy in positive ways.

- Engage with their play and their narratives. This will enable you to have a positive influence.

Wider issues for all children

"We were able to introduce shades of grey to the polarised media construct of good and bad.... model negotiation, prison or magic spells rather than violent death as punishment, and... challenge racist (good/white, bad/black) and helpless female stereotypes. In doing this we open the doors to other possible fantasy realms."

We Don't Play with Guns Here Penny Holland

- Where possible use the children's media interests as a stimulus for work across the areas of learning.
- Provide a discussion forum where children can talk about their media interests and display relevant accessories and toys. Appreciate and value the things that are important to them.
- Discuss and formulate a policy about gun play and superhero play.
- Look for ways in which children can have safe and positive experiences of media influences. Provide dressing up clothes and props and set clear boundaries for when and where they can be used. Consider designating a specific area for superhero play.
- Teach children how to resolve conflicts and ensure that all practitioners are consistent in their approach.

Conclusions

So what are the messages for practitioners working with young children, for their managers and for policy makers in local and national government?

One of the clearest messages is that boys and girls are <u>different</u>, their bodies and brains develop differently and at different rates. This means that the physical and educational needs of boys and girls are different, and trying to make them the same will not succeed.

> The workforce, which is predominantly female, must take time to find out how boys and girls develop, and incorporate this knowledge into their practice, provision and expectations of both boys and girls.
>
> Their managers must understand that boys and girls need different provision - not different equipment, but a modified approach both indoors and outside, so both boys and girls get what they need.
>
> Policy makers need to understand that a curriculum which favours the things that come easily and earlier to many girls may be just the curriculum which undermines the learning and motivation of many boys. A 'one size fits all' model where new initiatives are implemented and evaluated without much reference to the new research on brain development is doomed to failure. This model may fit some children, but many will experience only partial success, and a significant minority are in danger of suffering failure and a consequent loss of self esteem which will permanently and physically affect their brain structure, their ability to learn and their attitudes to education.

Another point for discussion and consideration is that although boys and girls are different, there is probably more difference within the sexes than between them!

The balance of <u>sex and gender</u> in each human varies (sex is in the perineum, gender is in the brain). Each of us seems to have a unique balance of masculine and feminine gender characteristics, although the vast majority of us are born with a clear physical sex. We must take this balance into account when making assumptions about 'all boys' and 'all girls' or 'all women' and 'all men'.

Practitioners and parents need to recognise that the children they live and work with are not stereotypical, they are unique. Each child (even brothers and sisters in the same family) has her or his own character, and we should take time to observe their behaviour to establish their needs and strengths.

There is a danger, both nationally and internationally, that in trying to ensure equality we are either trying to make boys more like girls, or give everyone exactly the same treatment. This has not worked and will not work! Boys' and girls' brains work differently, they are interested in different things, they learn in different ways and their bodies have different needs. Boys and girls see the world differently, respond to challenges differently and relate to others differently.

Practitioners need to find out more about the boys and girls in their care, looking at and for opportunities to meet the needs of both. This may mean challenging assumptions and stereotypes, changing attitudes to the needs of children, applying the knowledge we now have about learning, reorganising spaces and activities, and re-educating both the parents and the managers of early years settings. It may also mean changing some of the ways we model adult roles, provide activities, value different styles and places for learning, talk with and about children, and challenge all children.

In this short book, we have tried to cover a huge amount of research, theory, opinion and debate. We have tried to set this knowledge in the context of the early years curriculum, suggesting practical ways in which practitioners, teachers and parents can support the learning of all children, wherever they are on the gender spectrum and whatever their unique needs.

We hope you find the subject as fascinating as we do - our intention is to stimulate debate, support and expand current good practice, challenge stereotypical attitudes, and ensure that both boys and girls get the understanding they deserve. Research continues throughout the world, and will doubtless affect us in the future. Government policy responds only slowly to the issues raised by such research; in early years settings, we need to act immediately. Every girl and every boy passes our way only once, we must do what we know is right for each one.

Bibliography

Steve Biddulph	*Raising Boys*	0-00-715369-4	Thorsons
Nicola Call with	*The Thinking Child* and	1-855391-21-X	Network
Sally Featherstone	*The Thinking Child Resource Bk*	1-855391-61-9	Network
Various	*EPPE and REPPE reports*	Institute of Education, London	
Alison Gopnik et al	*How Babies Think*	0-75381-417-X	Phoenix
Daniel Goleman	*Emotional Intelligence*	0-7475-2830-6	Bloomsbury
Michael Gurian	*Boys & Girls Learn Differently*	0-7879-6117-5	Jossey-Bass
Vivian Gussin Paley	*Bad Guys Don't Have Birthdays*	0-226-64496-0	Chicago
Carla Hannaford	*Smart Moves*	0-915556-27-8	Great Ocean
Elizabeth Hartley-Brewer	*Raising Confident Girls*	1-55561-321-7	Da Capo
Elizabeth Hartley-Brewer	*Raising Confident Boys*	1-55561-320-9	Da Capo
Jane Healey	*Your Child's Growing Mind*	0-385-46930-6	Broadway
Penny Holland	*We Don't Play with Guns Here*	0-335-21089-9	Oxford UP
Ronald Kotulak	*Inside the Brain*	0-8362-3289-5	Andrews McMeel
Meggitt and Sutherland	*Child Development*	0-435-42056-9	Heinemann
Janet Moyles and Sian Adams	*Images of Violence*	1-905019-15-7	Featherstone
Lucinda Neall	*Bringing the Best Out in Boys*	1-903458-29-3	Hawthorn
NFER	*A Study of Transition from the Foundation Stage to Key Stage 1*	1-84478-441-X	DfES
Alistair Smith	*The Brain's Behind It*	1-85539-142-2	Network
Gordon Dryden & Jeannette Voss	*The Learning Revolution*	1-85539-085-X	Network
R L Welch and others	*Subtle Sex-role Cues in Children's Commercials*	Journal of Communication	

The contents of the the book have also been infomed by reading a range of articles and publications on the Internet sites of universities and other organisations across the world.